THIS COST ME SOMETHING

Because Nothing Worth Building Comes Free

By: Nikita Shumaker

Book One of the You Pay Either Way series

Dedication

This book was not written in isolation.

To my children, thank you for being my why on the days I wanted to stop and my reminder of what strength actually looks like. You taught me resilience without ever knowing you were teaching it. Everything I build is with you in mind.

To my husband, friends and family, thank you for standing beside me through the healing, the rebuilding, and the becoming. Your steadiness gave me room to find my voice again, and your belief in me mattered more than you know.

To my dad and sisters, thank you for being my steady since the beginning.

To my aunt, thank you for always encouraging me to write, even before I believed I could. Your faith in my words helped give this story a place to begin.

To the people who showed up quietly, consistently, and without needing to be asked, the ones who listened without fixing and stayed without questioning, thank you.

To the moments that required reflection, growth, and uncomfortable honesty, this book was shaped by them.

To the reader holding these pages, thank you for being here. If you see yourself in this book, know that you are not alone and you are not behind. Healing does not arrive all at once. It arrives in pieces, in pauses, and in the courage to keep going.

This cost me something.
This gave me something too.

For the price I am paying

And the version of me who stayed when it was hard

And the one who finally chose herself

Life charges interest on what we avoid

Contents

Closing: What Remains

Before You Go

Author's Note

This book is rooted in lived experience, reflection, and observation. While the themes are personal, the stories and examples have been shaped to protect privacy and create space for the reader to see themselves in the pages.

This is not a record of every detail, nor is it an attempt to assign blame or rewrite the past. It is an exploration of patterns, choices, and costs that often go unnoticed until they accumulate.

Some details have been changed. Some moments have been compressed. The truth of the experience remains.

This book is offered as an invitation to reflect, not a prescription for how to live. Take what resonates. Leave what does not. Trust your own awareness as you move forward.

Introduction

No one sets out to make the wrong choices. Most of us are doing the best we can with what we know, what we were taught, and what feels survivable in the moment. Decisions get made under pressure. Adaptation becomes instinct. Coping turns into routine. Life keeps moving whether we feel ready or not.

Somewhere along the way, we start paying for things we never remember agreeing to.

This book is not about dramatic mistakes or obvious failures. It is about the quiet costs. The ones that accumulate slowly enough to avoid detection. The ones that do not announce themselves as problems until they have already taken more than you expected.

This cost me something. Not in theory.
Not in hindsight.
In real life.

It cost me money I did not fully understand.
Time I did not get back.
Energy I thought I could replace later.
Pieces of myself I assumed would return once things settled down.

They did not.

What surprised me most was not the cost itself. It was how long I paid it without realizing I was paying at all. No warning showed up. No red flags waved dramatically. Nothing felt urgent enough to stop everything and reassess.

From the outside, life looked fine. Responsibilities were handled. Progress was being made. Stability appeared intact.

From the inside, something felt off.
Heavy.
Draining.
Unnamed.

I kept telling myself it was normal. That this was adulthood. That this was what commitment looked like. That everyone felt this way and learned to carry it.

That belief is expensive.

Most people are taught how to budget money. Few are taught how to recognize emotional debt. We learn how to be responsible long before we learn how to notice when responsibility quietly turns into self-sacrifice. We learn how to endure without being taught how to evaluate whether endurance is still necessary.

So we normalize the cost.

We stay quiet to keep the peace.

We delay decisions to avoid discomfort.

We trust systems without understanding the terms.

We choose familiar over aligned because familiar feels safer.

Each choice makes sense on its own. That is why the total is so shocking when it finally shows up.

This book exists because I needed language for what I was experiencing. Language to name the patterns that looked reasonable but felt wrong. Language to separate intention from consequence. Language to understand why being capable, responsible, and well-meaning still left me depleted.

Once language appeared, awareness followed. Once awareness followed, choice returned.

That is the work of this book.

Not to tell you what decisions to make.

Not to shame you for the ones you already made.

Not to promise an easy way out.

This is about recognition. It is about learning to see cost before it compounds. It is about understanding that every choice is a transaction whether you acknowledge it or not. It is about realizing that awareness does not remove responsibility, but it restores consent.

You will not find perfection here. You will find honesty. Real situations. Real patterns. Real consequences.

This is not a book written from a pedestal. It is written from lived experience, reflection, and the willingness to look directly at what something actually costs instead of what we hope it will cost.

If you have ever wondered why you feel tired in a way rest does not fix.
If you have ever looked at your life and thought nothing is technically wrong but something still feels heavy.
If you have ever delayed a decision because now did not feel like the right time and later arrived with interest.

You are not alone.
You are not failing.
You are becoming aware.

Life keeps score whether we look at it or not. This book is an invitation to look. To slow down long enough to ask what you are paying for. To decide whether the cost still makes sense. To choose intentionally instead of automatically.

Because once you see the receipt clearly, you get to decide what happens next.

That changes everything.

This book is about recognizing the costs you've been paying without consent and learning how to choose differently once you see them.

PART I

THE RECEIPT

Awareness

Before anything can change, it has to be seen.

Part I is about awareness.
Not dramatic realizations.
Not regret.
Recognition.

This section exists to name the quiet transactions that shape a life long before anyone calls them mistakes.

The costs that did not arrive all at once.
The decisions that never felt big enough to question.
The patterns that felt responsible, mature, or necessary at the time.

You just didn't know what you were funding.

I thought I was being responsible.
I thought I was easy to work with, easy to love, easy to keep around.
I didn't realize I was becoming too expensive to myself.

Part I is not about assigning blame.
It is about understanding how cost actually works when it stays invisible.

It hides in what feels normal.
It hides in what feels urgent.
It hides in silence, delay, convenience, and trust given without clarity.

This is where the receipt becomes visible.
Not to shame you.
Not to spiral you backward.
But to restore choice.

Once you see what is being charged quietly, you stop paying blindly.
You get to decide what continues.
What gets renegotiated.
What stops altogether.

Awareness does not remove cost.
It removes surprise.

This is where it begins.

CHAPTER ONE: This Cost Me Something

This cost me something.

Not in theory.
Not in hindsight.
In real life.

It cost me money I did not have.
Time I will never get back.
Lessons I learned without realizing I was enrolled.

The most expensive part was not what I lost.
It was what I did not realize I was paying for at the time.

That is how it usually happens.

The cost is not loud.
It does not arrive with flashing warnings or a final notice
stamped in red ink.
It slips in quietly, disguised as convenience, comfort, trust, or the
promise that it will work itself out later.

Later always comes.

When Cost Is Invisible

For a long time, I believed cost was something you calculated after the fact.

A mistake.

A bad investment.

A wrong turn.

Something you analyzed once the damage was done.

What I did not understand was this.

Every decision carries a price.

Even the ones you do not realize you are making.

Especially those.

Most of us were never taught how to evaluate cost beyond money.

We learned price tags, monthly payments, and interest rates.

We learned how to stretch a dollar without learning how to recognize when something was quietly draining us dry.

No one explained the cost of silence.

The cost of staying.

The cost of avoiding uncomfortable conversations.

The cost of handing over responsibility because someone else sounded more confident.

We were told to trust the process.

Trust the system.

Trust that things would work out.

What no one mentioned was that trust without awareness is still a transaction.

Life keeps score.

Cost becomes invisible in two ways.

Sometimes it hides inside what feels normal.

Sometimes it hides inside what feels urgent.

Normal is the easiest disguise.

Normal makes you stop asking questions.

Normal teaches you to accept ongoing charges as if they are just part of being an adult.

Urgency is the second disguise.

Urgency convinces you that speed matters more than clarity.

Urgency pushes you to sign, agree, comply, commit, move on.

Urgency rarely asks whether the price is fair.

Urgency just wants the situation over with.

That is how a lot of people end up paying for things they never would have chosen with a clear mind.

The Slow Accumulation

At some point, almost everyone has a moment where they look around and wonder how they got there.

Not because of one catastrophic choice.

Because of a hundred small ones that never felt urgent enough to question.

The job that slowly consumed your health.

The relationship that required you to shrink in order to keep the peace.

The financial decision you did not question because asking felt embarrassing.

The delay you justified because you were almost ready.

Almost is expensive.

The bill does not come all at once.

It arrives in installments.

Late nights.

Missed moments.

Lingering anxiety.

A quiet resentment that is difficult to name.

By the time you notice, you have already paid more than you intended.

The slow accumulation is what makes cost so hard to confront.

No single charge feels big enough to call a meeting about.

No single moment feels dramatic enough to justify change.

The weight is built quietly.

I used to believe that if something was truly wrong, it would feel obvious.
It would demand attention loudly.
It would come with a clear warning.

Most of the time, it does not.
Most of the time, it just becomes your routine.

A Moment That Looked Harmless

There was a time when I realized I had been saying yes on autopilot.

Not because it aligned.
Not because it made sense.
Because explaining a no felt heavier than living with the cost.

In the moment, it felt practical.
It felt mature.
It felt like choosing peace.

What it actually was, was deferred discomfort.

That decision did not explode immediately.
Nothing dramatic happened.
Life continued as if nothing had shifted.

Months later, I noticed how tired I was.
Not the kind of tired sleep fixes.

The kind that settles into your posture.
The kind that makes you guarded without realizing it.
The kind that shortens your patience and dulls your curiosity.

That was the cost showing up late.

The hardest part of moments like this is that they rarely feel
wrong while you are in them.
They feel like compromise.
They feel like being the bigger person.
They feel like responsibility.

I remember sitting with that tiredness and trying to solve it like a
puzzle.
I adjusted my schedule.
I tried to rest more.
I told myself I just needed a reset.

The reset never lasted.

The truth was uncomfortable.
The tiredness was not from doing too much.
The tiredness was from carrying too much that was not mine to
carry.

There was another time when I said yes because I did not want to appear difficult.
The request was not outrageous.
It was framed as simple.
It was presented as the easiest path forward.

The kind of request that makes hesitation feel unnecessary and questions feel inconvenient.

I agreed quickly, then felt the discomfort later.

That discomfort was not anxiety for no reason.
It was my intuition noticing that I had just accepted terms I had not fully examined.

Not because I could not.
Because slowing down felt socially expensive.

I remember thinking about how often I did that.
How often I chose speed over clarity.
How often I relied on other people to define what was reasonable.
How often I confused confidence with correctness.

That was when I understood something I had not wanted to admit.

Avoiding discomfort does not eliminate it.
Avoiding discomfort reschedules it.

The future version of you always gets the appointment.

Intention Does Not Cancel Consequence

We like to believe intention is what matters most.
As long as we meant well, the outcome should reflect that.

Intention does not cancel consequence.

You can mean well and still end up depleted.
You can try your best and still realize your best was uninformed.
You can love deeply and still lose yourself in the process.

That does not make you careless.
It makes you human.

The problem is not that we make mistakes.
The problem is that we refuse to examine the cost until it hurts
enough to demand attention.

There is a difference between a mistake and a pattern.
Mistakes happen.
Patterns repeat.

Patterns repeat because they stay unnamed.
They stay unnamed because naming them requires
accountability.

Accountability is uncomfortable when you are already stretched
thin.
That discomfort is often what keeps people paying the same cost
for years.

The Myth of Readiness

There is a quiet myth many of us grow up with.
The belief that clarity comes before action.
The belief that one day you will feel ready.
The belief that confidence will show up first.

That day rarely comes.

Most real decisions happen while you are unsure.
While you are tired.
While you are managing responsibilities that do not pause.

So you choose the familiar.
You choose what keeps things calm for now.
You tell yourself you will revisit it later.

Later is never neutral.

Readiness is often described like it is a switch.
One day it will flip.
One day you will feel certain.

Real life rarely offers certainty.
It offers pressure.

Pressure does not wait for readiness.
Pressure asks you to choose anyway.

That is why awareness matters more than readiness.

Responsibility Without Blame

For a long time, responsibility felt like blame.
If something went wrong, someone had to be at fault.

Acknowledging my role felt like failure.
Avoiding ownership felt safer.

That avoidance did not protect me.
It kept me stuck.

Ownership is not about punishment.
It is about power.

Once you own the outcome, patterns become visible.
Once patterns are visible, they can be changed.

Ownership does not mean you caused everything.
Ownership means you stop pretending you have no influence.

That shift is subtle.
That shift is everything.

It is the difference between repeating a life and building one.

Pause

Take a moment before moving on.

Name one quiet, ongoing cost you feel in your life right now.
Notice how it shows up in your energy, focus, or mood.
Notice what it asks of you each week.
Consider what this would cost you five years from now if
nothing changed.

Choosing With Awareness

This book is not about regret.
It is about recognition.

It is about looking at your life honestly and saying,
This is what it is costing me.

Not to judge yourself.
Not to spiral.
To wake up.

When you understand that every choice is a transaction, you start asking better questions.

What am I paying for this peace.
What am I giving up to stay comfortable.
What is this silence really costing me over time.
Is this a price I am willing to keep paying.

Some costs are worth it.
Growth costs something.
Healing costs something.
Building something better often costs more up front than staying where you are.

Those costs are intentional.
They move you forward.

The dangerous ones are the costs you never name.
The ones that drain you quietly.
The ones you justify because they do not hurt all at once.

Those are the ones that leave you wondering how you lost so much without ever feeling like you chose to.

Awareness does not remove cost.
Awareness changes the direction of your payment.

You stop paying for avoidance.
You start paying for alignment.

That is a trade worth making.

Reflect

Name one cost you have been absorbing without consent.
Notice how it shows up.
Notice what it asks of you.
Notice what it gives back.

Consider what it would look like to stop paying it quietly.

This Is Where It Begins

If you are reading this, something has already asked for payment.

Maybe it was a financial wake-up call.
A relationship that forced clarity.
An exhaustion you cannot push through anymore.
A realization that the life you are building does not match the
one you imagined.

You are not behind.
You are becoming aware.

This is a space for real conversations.
About decisions made without full information.

About money we did not fully understand.

About relationships that taught us more than we wanted to learn.

About building something better while still figuring it out.

No hype.

No shame.

Just truth, growth, and forward motion.

Life keeps score.

Once you see the cost clearly, you get to decide what you are willing to pay next.

CHAPTER TWO: Not in Theory. In Real Life.

In theory, most decisions are simple.

You gather information.
You weigh the options.
You wait until you feel confident.
You choose the best path.

In theory, people communicate clearly.
Money behaves predictably.
Effort is rewarded.
Good intentions lead to good outcomes.

In theory, there is time.

Real life does not operate on theory.

In real life, decisions arrive without warning.
They show up while you are busy, tired, distracted, or already overwhelmed.
They do not wait for clarity.
They do not pause until you feel ready.

They ask anyway.

When Decisions Do Not Wait

Most defining choices are made in imperfect conditions.

You decide without knowing everything.
You commit while still carrying doubt.
You stay because leaving feels disruptive.
You leave because staying costs too much of who you are.

There is rarely a clean moment where all the variables line up and the answer becomes obvious.

What exists instead is pressure.

Pressure to decide.
Pressure to keep things moving.
Pressure to not disappoint.
Pressure to prove you can handle it.

Pressure convinces you that choosing quickly is better than choosing carefully.

Later, when the cost becomes visible, you wonder how you missed it.

Most people do not miss it because they are careless.
They miss it because life is loud.

Responsibilities stack.
People need things.
The day moves fast.

The mind prioritizes what feels urgent over what feels important.

That is how expensive decisions get made in ordinary moments.

Reasonable Choices Can Be Expensive

We like to believe costly decisions come from recklessness.
Most of them do not.

They come from practicality.
From trust.
From trying to manage too many responsibilities at once.

They come from believing you are being mature by staying calm
and keeping things moving.

You trusted someone who sounded confident.
You agreed without fully understanding because asking felt
uncomfortable.
You delayed action because everything else felt more urgent.

None of that feels irresponsible in the moment.
It feels manageable.

Manageable choices often become expensive ones over time.

A choice can be reasonable and still cost too much.
A choice can make sense and still be misaligned.

A choice can keep the peace today and create a bill you cannot afford tomorrow.

The Cost of Delay

Delay rarely looks like refusal.
Delay looks like not yet.

Not yet when things calm down.
Not yet until the next paycheck.
Not yet until you have more information.
Not yet until you feel stronger.

Delay often feels wise.
It can sound like patience.
It can sound like restraint.
It can look like you are being responsible by not rushing.

Delay is sometimes wisdom.
Delay is sometimes fear with better branding.

The difference shows up later.

If delay gives you clarity, it was preparation.
If delay gives you more anxiety and fewer options, it was avoidance.

A Moment That Did Not Feel Urgent

There was a time when I delayed a decision because nothing felt wrong enough to demand attention.

Nothing was broken.
Nothing required immediate action.
Everything appeared stable.

The issue stayed in the background.
I noticed it.
I acknowledged it.
I told myself I would deal with it once things slowed down.

Things never slowed down.

Weeks passed.
Then months.

When action was finally unavoidable, the options were fewer and the cost was higher.

What could have been a thoughtful decision became a reactive one.

The delay did not remove the cost.
The delay increased it.

The most frustrating part was not the expense itself.
The most frustrating part was the realization that earlier me could have afforded this, emotionally and practically.

Later me had to pay for the same decision while already depleted.

Delay does not pause life.
Delay lets life choose the terms.

The Cost of Reaction

Living in reaction mode creates a specific kind of exhaustion.

Constantly responding instead of choosing.
Managing consequences instead of shaping direction.
Making decisions based on what causes the least disruption right now.

Reaction feels necessary at times.
Some seasons require it.

When reaction becomes habitual, the cost compounds.

You wake up one day realizing your life has been shaped more by urgency than intention.

Urgency is expensive.

Urgency steals time from the decisions that deserve it.
Urgency narrows your options.
Urgency turns your values into afterthoughts.

A rushed yes can cost more than a thoughtful no ever would.

Pause

Take a moment before moving on.

Name one area where urgency has been choosing for you.
Notice what decision felt rushed because slowing down felt inconvenient.
Notice what you have been managing instead of choosing.

Consider what you would decide if urgency was removed.

Neutrality Is a Myth

Being unprepared does not exempt you from outcomes.

No discount exists because no one taught you.
No exemption applies because you were doing your best.

Life is not cruel for this.
It is neutral.

Avoiding a decision does not remove the cost.
Avoiding a decision delays it.

Delayed costs almost always arrive with interest.

Interest does not always look like money.

Interest looks like stress.

Interest looks like regret.

Interest looks like fewer options and tighter timelines.

Interest looks like the moment you realize you waited so long that you no longer get to choose from the same menu.

Hindsight Is Not the Teacher

Hindsight feels sharp because it arrives after payment.

Looking back makes old decisions feel obvious.
That clarity was not available at the time.

The work is not self-punishment.
The work is pattern recognition.

The better question is not, why did I fail.
The better question is, why did this choice make sense to me in that moment.

That question reveals beliefs.

Beliefs about safety.
Beliefs about worth.
Beliefs about what you were allowed to want.
Beliefs about what you thought you had to tolerate.

Those beliefs shape decisions long before logic arrives.

Reflect

Name one decision you delayed that is still active in your life.
Notice how that delay shows up.
Notice what it asks of you now that it did not ask of you earlier.
Notice what continuing to wait protects you from facing.

Consider what the delay is costing you quietly.

Awareness Changes the Transaction

This book does not exist to tell you what choices to make.
It exists to help you recognize when you are paying for
something you did not mean to buy.

Awareness changes the transaction.

You may still choose stability.
You may still choose patience.
You may still choose familiarity.

The difference is that the choice becomes intentional.

Not accidental.
Not automatic.
Not built on pressure.

What Comes Next

The next chapter moves beyond individual decisions into accumulation.

Emotional debt.
Financial debt.
Relational debt.

The quiet scoreboard no one talks about.

CHAPTER THREE: Life Keeps Score

Most people do not notice when the score starts adding up.

There is no announcement.

No checkpoint.

No moment where someone tells you where you stand.

Life does not pause to review totals.

It records quietly.

The Score You Do Not See

We tend to expect consequences to arrive dramatically.

A sudden loss.

A visible failure.

A breaking point that demands attention.

More often, consequence looks like accumulation.

A little more exhaustion than last year.

A little less patience than you used to have.

A low-level anxiety you cannot trace to one event.

Nothing feels catastrophic.

Just heavier.

The danger is not always in the event.
The danger is in the slow normalization.

People adapt to what they carry.
The body adjusts.
The mind learns to function while burdened.
The heart learns to keep moving even when it feels misaligned.

Survival is impressive.
Survival is not free.

Emotional Debt

Emotional debt builds when you keep absorbing what you never agreed to carry.

It builds when you keep showing up as the strong one without being supported.
It builds when you keep minimizing your own needs because someone else has bigger feelings.
It builds when you keep telling yourself you are fine, then silently resent the people who believe you.

Emotional debt rarely shows up as a single collapse.

It shows up as irritability.
It shows up as numbness.
It shows up as the inability to feel joy the way you used to.

It shows up as being touched out, talked out, tired of explaining, tired of being responsible.

Financial Debt

Financial debt is obvious in numbers.
Emotional debt is obvious in patterns.

Financial debt often begins the same way emotional debt begins.

One decision that felt necessary.
One delay that felt manageable.
One agreement made quickly because slowing down felt expensive.

Debt is not always irresponsibility.
Debt is often pressure meeting limited options.

The question is not whether debt exists.
The question is whether the pattern behind it stays unnamed.

Relational Debt

Relational debt builds when repair does not happen.

It builds when resentment stays unspoken.
It builds when someone gets used to your silence.
It builds when you keep tolerating what you would never advise someone else to tolerate.

Relationships keep score in small ways.

Not always with revenge.
Sometimes with distance.

Distance looks like less laughter.
Distance looks like guarded conversations.
Distance looks like a home that functions but no longer feels safe.

Surviving Versus Building

There is a difference between surviving and building.

Survival focuses on today.
Keeping things from falling apart.
Managing the immediate.
Getting everyone through the week.

Building requires margin.
Choices made with tomorrow in mind.
Boundaries that protect the future version of you.
Decisions that cost more up front because they buy you peace later.

Survival has a place.
When survival becomes the long-term strategy, the cost shows up later.

In your body.

In your finances.

In your relationships.

Endurance without direction is expensive.

What You Tolerate Sets the Score

Most people underestimate the cost of what they tolerate.

They tell themselves it is temporary.
They assume it is not that bad.

Tolerance sets a standard.

What you allow repeatedly becomes what life assumes you are willing to carry.
Life will let you carry it for a very long time.

A Quiet Realization

There was a point when I realized rest was no longer fixing the tiredness.

Sleep helped briefly.
Time off helped temporarily.

The heaviness returned.

What I noticed was not one problem.
It was accumulation.

Small compromises.
Unspoken boundaries.
Delayed decisions.

Each one felt manageable.
Together, they were expensive.

There is a specific kind of frustration that comes with this
realization.

You start looking for the one thing to fix.
You start thinking a vacation will solve it.
You start believing productivity is the answer.

The body keeps returning the same message.

This is not a rest problem.
This is a cost problem.

Pause

Take a moment before moving on.

Name one thing that feels manageable but constant.
Notice what drains you without demanding attention.
Notice what you have normalized that feels heavier over time.

Consider what this cost would look like if it continued unchanged.

Where Resentment Begins

Resentment rarely comes from nowhere.

It grows when you keep paying for something you never consciously agreed to.

Resentment is not failure.
Resentment is information.

It signals misalignment.

Ignoring it does not remove it.
Ignoring it adds interest.

Stability Can Be Expensive

Some of the highest costs come from not moving at all.

Staying because leaving feels disruptive.
Maintaining dynamics that require constant self-sacrifice.
Protecting systems that drain you because you helped build them.

Stability built on avoidance carries interest.
The longer you stay, the higher the bill becomes.

Awareness Stops the Bleeding

Awareness does not erase past costs.
Awareness stops unnecessary ones.

Once you see where energy is leaking, you can interrupt the pattern.

You do not need to change everything.
You need to notice what keeps charging you without return.

That is what Part I is doing.

It is showing you the scoreboard.
It is handing you the receipt.
It is giving you language for what you already feel.

What Comes Next

The interlude that follows is not extra.
It is your hinge.

It names the moment when you realize you have been paying without consent.
It prepares you for Part II, where patterns stop being abstract and start becoming visible.

INTERLUDE: An Account You Didn't Know You Opened

There is a moment most people recognize only in hindsight.

Not when something breaks.
Not when everything falls apart.

Earlier than that.

It happens when you realize you have been carrying something for a long time without remembering when you agreed to it.

The realization is rarely dramatic.
It does not announce itself with a clear event.

It shows up quietly.

You notice irritation where patience used to be.
You feel unusually drained by conversations that once felt neutral.
You rest, but the tiredness stays.

You keep functioning, but something feels off.

Nothing is technically wrong.
Life still works.

Bills get paid.

Responsibilities get handled.

People rely on you.

That is what makes the moment unsettling.

If nothing is wrong, why does everything feel so heavy?

For a long time, I assumed that heaviness meant I needed to manage better.

Be more efficient.

Be more disciplined.

Be more grateful.

I adjusted schedules.

Streamlined commitments.

Optimized routines.

Pushed through.

The heaviness stayed.

What I did not understand yet was this.

I was not tired from effort.

I was tired from carrying costs I had never acknowledged.

It is easy to miss the moment these accounts open.

They do not feel like decisions.
They feel like survival.

You say yes because it avoids conflict.
You stay quiet because speaking feels risky.
You accept terms because questioning them feels inconvenient
or embarrassing.
You delay action because everything else feels louder.

Each choice feels reasonable.
Each one feels small.

None of them come with paperwork.

No one tells you that you have agreed to recurring charges.
No one hands you a breakdown of emotional interest rates.
No one explains how deferred decisions compound over time.

Life continues.
The account stays open.

Over time, the charges change shape.

What started as flexibility becomes obligation.
What started as patience becomes self-erasure.
What started as trust becomes disengagement.

The shift does not announce itself.

It becomes noticeable when you stop recognizing yourself in your reactions.

Tolerance drops.
Frustration rises.
The body signals before the mind catches up.

That is when the internal audit begins.

Conversations replay.
Decisions get revisited.
Questions surface about why things that once felt manageable now feel suffocating.

An uncomfortable truth slowly emerges.

Payment has been happening without conscious agreement.

This did not happen because of carelessness.
It happened because language was missing.

Most people were taught how to pay bills.
Few were taught how to recognize emotional debt.

Responsibility was modeled.
The quiet slide into self-sacrifice was not explained.

Endurance was praised.
Evaluation of whether endurance was still necessary was not.

Charges became normalized.

This gets called adulthood.
This gets described as commitment.
This gets framed as stability.

Normalization is powerful.

Once a cost becomes familiar, alarms stop sounding.
Once alarms stop sounding, the cost starts shaping a life.

Standards adjust.
Expectations shrink.
The nervous system adapts to depletion.

From the outside, nothing looks broken.
From the inside, constant compensation is happening.

This is how quiet misalignment lasts for years.

Not because awareness is absent.
Because awareness was never named.

There is a moment, if attention is present, when awareness
finally lands.

The moment is subtle.

Anger shows up where it does not belong.
Resentment appears without a clear source.
Grief surfaces for a version of yourself you did not realize was slipping away.

That moment is not failure.
That moment is the receipt.

It is the point where life shows the total so far.

The purpose is not punishment.
The purpose is information.

A simple question gets asked.

Are you willing to keep paying this?

Most people do not answer immediately.

Minimization follows.
Rationalization steps in.
Temporary explanations take over.

Temporary costs become permanent when they are never named.

Naming changes the transaction.

Once a cost is named, it stops operating in the background.
It becomes visible.

It becomes negotiable.
It becomes optional.

Payment may still continue.
That part matters.

Awareness does not remove obligation.
Awareness restores consent.

There are seasons when carrying more is a choice.

Energy gets invested.
Discomfort gets absorbed.

Those choices feel different when they are intentional.

The most dangerous costs are the ones never chosen.

Inherited costs.
Assumed costs.
Defaulted costs.

These drain quietly while presenting themselves as normal.

This book exists to interrupt that pattern.

Not to dictate what should stop.
Not to prescribe immediate action.

To help you recognize when a charge is occurring.

Clarity changes what happens next.

The decision to keep paying, renegotiate, or close the account entirely belongs to you.

What Comes Next

Part I made the transaction visible.

Part II looks at how these accounts stay open.

The patterns that feel responsible.
The behaviors that once protected you.
The costs that look polite, loving, or mature.

Because the most expensive things in life rarely ask for payment up front.
They simply keep score.

PART II

THE INVISIBLE COSTS

Patterns

The most expensive things rarely come with a price tag.

Most people do not get stuck because they are reckless.
They get stuck because their patterns once made sense.

Part I was about awareness.
Seeing the receipt.
Recognizing that life had been charging quietly for longer than
you realized.

Part II is about patterns.

Patterns are where cost becomes normalized.
Where decisions stop feeling like decisions.
Where behavior repeats without needing explanation.

These are the costs that feel responsible.
Polite.
Even loving.

They rarely look like mistakes.
They look like maturity.

This section exists to make those patterns visible.

Not to shame them.
To interrupt them.

Because once you can see the pattern, you are no longer trapped inside it.

CHAPTER FOUR: Costs That Can't Be Bought or Sold

Some of the most expensive things in life never show up on a statement.

They do not have price tags.
They do not come with invoices.
They are not tracked in neat columns or monthly totals.

They are paid for in quieter ways.

In energy.
In emotional capacity.
In self-trust.
In how much of yourself you bring into rooms before you start holding parts back.

Because these costs cannot be measured easily, they are often dismissed.

That dismissal is costly.

You cannot budget what you refuse to name.
You cannot protect what you pretend is free.

These costs do not arrive as emergencies.
They arrive as expectations.

When the Cost Feels Like Being Needed

Most people do not realize they are paying these costs because they feel like virtues.

Being dependable.
Being emotionally available.
Being flexible.
Being capable.

You are the one people lean on.
The one who adapts.
The one who keeps things steady when others fall apart.

From the outside, this looks like strength.
From the inside, it often feels like constant readiness.

You stay alert.
You anticipate needs.
You adjust before anyone has to ask.

Nothing collapses.
That becomes the proof that it is manageable.

The cost stays invisible because the system keeps working.

When Strength Becomes the Currency

Strength is often treated like a renewable resource.

If you have handled things before, you are expected to handle them again.

If you stayed calm once, calm becomes your role.

If you adapted quickly, adaptation becomes the baseline.

The transaction is subtle.

You are trusted because you are capable.

You are leaned on because you are steady.

You are not checked on because you seem fine.

No one announces that this is the deal.

It just becomes normal.

Strength without reciprocity drains.

Not dramatically.

Gradually.

You do not notice it leaving all at once.

You notice it in shorter patience.

In hesitation when someone asks for one more thing.

In the quiet relief you feel when plans get canceled.

The cost shows up as depletion long before it shows up as collapse.

Emotional Availability Has a Bill

Emotional availability is rarely tracked.

Listening does not leave a paper trail.
Holding space does not generate receipts.
Absorbing tension does not show up on a ledger.

So it feels endless.

You show up.
You respond.
You reassure.
You regulate.

Nothing breaks.

Over time, something thins.

You notice yourself holding back reactions.
You notice irritation where patience used to live.
You notice fatigue that rest does not fully resolve.

The cost is not visible to anyone else.
It is internal.

And because it is internal, it is easy to minimize.

Why These Costs Last So Long

Costs that cannot be bought or sold are the ones people pay the longest.

Because no one taught you how to recognize them.
Because they are framed as character traits instead of expenses.
Because questioning them feels selfish or ungrateful.

If you grew up watching people absorb quietly, absorbing feels normal.
If responsibility was praised without relief following it, endurance feels expected.
If being capable kept things stable, capability becomes your entry fee.

These costs do not feel chosen.
They feel assumed.

And assumed costs rarely get examined.

The Accumulation You Feel Before You Understand

Unlike financial costs, these do not trigger alarms.

There is no overdraft notice for emotional depletion.
No statement that shows when self-trust begins to erode.
No warning when flexibility turns into self-erasure.

The accumulation is felt before it is understood.

Irritation without a clear source.
Resistance to being asked for anything else.
A quiet grief for a version of yourself that felt more present.

Nothing about this feels dramatic.
Which is why it lasts.

Naming Without Fixing

This chapter is not here to tell you how to stop giving.
It is not here to instruct you on boundaries.
It is not here to rebalance anything.

It is here to name what often goes unnamed.

To recognize that not all costs are financial.
That not all expenses are visible.
That not all strength is free.

Awareness does not eliminate these costs.
It changes their status.

Once something is named, it stops operating in the background.

That matters.

Pause

Before moving on, notice what registered.

Notice which costs felt familiar.
Notice which ones you recognized immediately.
Notice which lines made you uncomfortable.

Pay attention to what your body did as you read this.

Recognition often arrives quietly.

Reflect

Name one cost in your life that cannot be bought or sold.

Not one that feels dramatic.
One that feels normal.

Notice how it shows up in your energy.
In your availability.
In how much of yourself you bring into rooms.

Notice whether that cost is acknowledged by anyone else.
Notice whether it has ever been named as a cost at all..

This is not about fixing.
It is about seeing clearly what has been carried.

What remains invisible is the easiest to inherit.

CHAPTER FIVE: The Cost of Comfort

Comfort is rarely free.

It simply spreads the payment out slowly enough that you stop noticing.

At first, comfort feels like relief.

It feels like safety.

It feels like choosing calm over chaos.

Comfort looks responsible.

It looks mature.

It looks like stability.

That is why it is so easy to justify.

When Comfort Looks Like Stability

Comfort rarely shows up as indulgence.

It shows up as familiarity.

Staying where you already know the rules.

Choosing what does not require explanation.

Accepting what is predictable, even when it is limiting.

Comfort feels like control.

Control feels like security.

Security feels like safety.

Until you notice what you traded to get it.

Comfort becomes dangerous when it is mistaken for alignment.

When staying feels virtuous simply because leaving would be disruptive.

When endurance is praised more than honesty.

The Deal You Did Not Realize You Made

Most people do not stay stuck because they love where they are.

They stay because leaving feels expensive.

Leaving costs energy.

Leaving costs uncertainty.

Leaving costs being misunderstood.

Staying costs less up front.

So people stay and call it patience.

They call it loyalty.

They call it being practical.

Patience without direction slowly becomes avoidance.

Comfort often asks for small compromises.

Truth for peacekeeping.
Growth for stability.
Curiosity for certainty.

Each compromise feels manageable.
Together, they become costly.

A Choice That Felt Responsible

There was a time when staying felt like the mature decision.

Nothing was technically wrong.
Nothing demanded urgency.
Everything looked fine from the outside.

Leaving would have raised questions.
Staying required silence.

Silence felt easier.

Over time, I noticed how much energy went into maintaining comfort.
How often I edited myself.
How little room there was to breathe.

Comfort had not protected me.
It had reduced me.

The Erosion of Self-Trust

One of the quietest costs of comfort is self-betrayal.

The moments when you know better and choose easier.
The conversations you rehearse and never have.
The boundaries you soften because holding them feels
exhausting.

Each moment feels small.
Together, they erode trust with yourself.

Rebuilding that trust costs more than protecting it ever would
have.

Pause

Take a moment before moving on.

Name one place where you have chosen comfort over alignment.
Notice what feels stable while quietly draining you.
Notice what you are maintaining that requires you to stay
smaller.

Consider what truth you would tell if comfort was no longer the
goal.

Comfort Versus Alignment

Comfort often disguises itself as loyalty.

Staying because you have always stayed.
Protecting systems you helped build.
Remaining silent to avoid shifting a dynamic.

Loyalty has value.
Loyalty that requires you to disappear does not.

Comfort shrinks your world quietly.

You stop asking certain questions.
You stop imagining alternatives.
You stop challenging what no longer fits.

Not because you do not notice.
Because noticing would require change.

Reflect

Name one area where comfort has replaced honesty.
Notice how it shows up in your choices and your self-talk.
Notice what it asks of you long term and what it gives back.

Consider what it would look like to stop paying for comfort
quietly.

Choosing Comfort Consciously

Comfort is not the enemy.

Rest matters.
Stability matters.
Ease matters.

Comfort without awareness becomes costly.

The question is not whether change will cost you something.
It will.

The question is whether staying exactly where you are is quietly
costing you more.

CHAPTER SIX: The Cost of Silence

Silence is rarely neutral.

It looks passive.
It feels controlled.
It is often praised as maturity.

Silence is a choice.
Every choice carries a cost.

When Silence Feels Safer

Most people do not stay silent because they have nothing to say.
They stay silent because saying it feels risky.

Risky to the relationship.
Risky to the dynamic.
Risky to the version of peace they worked hard to maintain.

So they smooth it over.
They hold it in.
They tell themselves it is not worth the tension.

In the moment, that feels true.

Silence Is Not Kindness

Silence is often framed as kindness.

Do not upset them.

Do not make it awkward.

Do not create a problem.

Kindness that consistently excludes you is not kindness.
It is self-abandonment.

Many people learned early that speaking came with
consequences.

Dismissal.
Being labeled difficult.
Being told they were too much.

What protected you once can imprison you later.

The Internal Cost

Silence does not remove conflict.
It relocates it.

It settles in the body.
In the chest.
In the jaw.
In the fatigue that does not lift.

Repeated silence creates distance.

Between what you think and what you say.
Between what you feel and what you express.

Over time, that distance becomes expensive.

A Pattern That Felt Like Strength

There was a season when staying quiet felt like maturity.

Speaking up created friction.
Silence kept things calm.

I told myself it was temporary.

The tension showed up anyway.
It just showed up inward.

I felt unseen while being present.
Resentful while being agreeable.

Silence preserved the dynamic.
It did not preserve me.

Pause

Take a moment before moving on.

Name one place where you stay silent to keep things smooth.
Notice what truth you keep postponing.
Notice what the silence costs you internally.

Consider what you would say if peace did not require self-erasure.

When Silence Becomes Habit

The first time you stay quiet, it feels intentional.
The tenth time, it feels familiar.
Eventually, it feels automatic.

People get used to you not pushing back.
Not asking for more.
Not challenging the status quo.

When you finally speak, it feels disruptive.

Not because it is.
Because it breaks a pattern you helped create.

Reflect

Name one thing you have not said to protect peace.
Notice how that silence shows up in your body and your patience.

Notice what it requires you to swallow and what it teaches others to expect.

Consider what it would look like to stop paying for silence quietly.

Speaking does not guarantee agreement.
Silence guarantees one outcome.

Nothing changes.

Alignment requires voice.
Delay is never free.

CHAPTER SEVEN: The Cost of Indifference

Indifference is not always loud.
It does not always arrive as cruelty.

Sometimes it arrives as the slow removal of care.

It is the unanswered question that stays unanswered.
The conversation that never gets revisited.
The look that does not land.
The effort that quietly stops, then gets treated like that is normal.

Indifference rarely gives you a clean reason to leave.
That is why it is so expensive.

When something is clearly wrong, your body responds.

You name it.
You brace.
You adjust.
You make decisions.

Indifference does not trigger the same alarms.
It creates a fog.

You are still in the room, but you are no longer being met there.
You are still showing up, but the weight is not shared.

You are still trying, but the relationship, the system, the agreement is no longer trying back.

Nothing breaks in one moment.
Everything just becomes heavier.

The Cost of Being Unmissed

There is a specific kind of pain that comes from realizing you could disappear emotionally and nothing would shift.

Not because people are evil.
Because they are comfortable.
Because they have adjusted to you carrying the temperature of everything.

You become the one who notices.
The one who remembers.
The one who brings the energy.
The one who repairs the tone after conflict.
The one who asks the follow-up questions.
The one who keeps the connection alive.

Indifference teaches you to work for basic engagement.

It turns love into labor.
It turns partnership into management.

It teaches you to over-function.

You start filling the gaps automatically.
You start anticipating disappointment.
You start explaining things away before you even allow yourself to feel them.

You stop expecting effort because expecting effort hurts.

That is the first cost.

Lowered expectation.

Lowered expectation looks like maturity from the outside.
It is often grief on the inside.

How Indifference Hides

Indifference is hard to confront because it does not always look like neglect.

Sometimes it looks like busy.
Sometimes it looks like stress.
Sometimes it looks like personality.

Sometimes it looks like a person who says the right things and does none of them.
Sometimes it looks like someone who is present physically but absent relationally.

You can share space with someone every day and still feel alone.

Indifference can live inside routines.

Meals.
Schedules.
Bills.
A life that functions.

Functioning is not intimacy.
Functioning is not care.
Functioning is not being chosen.

A home can run like a machine while a relationship dies quietly inside it.

That is why indifference lasts.
Because everything still works.

The Effort Becomes One-Sided

At first, you try to fix it the way responsible people fix things.

You communicate more clearly.
You soften your tone.
You choose your timing carefully.
You ask for simple things instead of big things.

You do not ask for miracles.

You ask for presence.
For curiosity.
For a response that feels like you matter.

When indifference is present, even small requests feel like burdens to the other person.

You can feel it.

You begin managing your needs so they do not inconvenience anyone.
You start editing your disappointment.
You stop bringing things up because the reaction costs more than the issue.

You begin paying for peace with self-erasure.

Indifference does not just remove effort from the other person.
It removes voice from you.

The Cost of Explaining It to Yourself

One of the most expensive parts of indifference is the internal negotiation it creates.

You start talking yourself out of what you see.

Maybe I am being dramatic.
Maybe I am asking for too much.

Maybe they are just tired.
Maybe this is normal.

You start building a case against your own instincts.

Indifference makes you question whether your needs are valid
because there is no clear offense to point to.

No obvious betrayal.
No headline.

Just absence.

Absence is hard to defend.

You feel lonely, then feel guilty for feeling lonely.
You feel disappointed, then feel immature for wanting more.
You feel the distance, then convince yourself you should be
grateful things are not worse.

That is how people stay.

Not because they do not know.
Because they cannot prove it.

Indifference turns your life into a courtroom where your feelings
are always on trial.

The Emotional Interest Rate

Indifference charges interest.

It charges interest on every unasked question.

Every unspoken need.

Every moment you swallow the truth to keep things smooth.

The interest looks like resentment.

It looks like numbness.

It looks like being irritated by things that should not feel that big.

It looks like your nervous system staying alert even when nothing is happening.

It looks like you feeling alone even when you are not.

Indifference makes joy feel unsafe because joy requires presence.

It requires being met.

It requires trust that the moment will be shared.

When you are used to carrying everything alone, even happiness feels like work.

The Slow Death of Repair

The clearest sign of indifference is not conflict.

It is the absence of repair.

Conflict is normal.

Missteps happen.

Stress exists.

Repair is what tells you the connection still matters.

Repair is the follow-up conversation.

Repair is the accountability without defensiveness.

Repair is the willingness to revisit something because you care about how it landed.

Indifference does not repair.

It moves on.

It lets time do the job that honesty should do.

It lets you carry what should have been shared.

It teaches you that bringing things up makes you the problem.

Over time, you stop trying.

Not because you stop caring.

Because caring alone hurts.

Pause

Name one place in your life where indifference has been present.

Not anger.

Not conflict.

Absence.

Notice what stopped happening.

The check-ins.

The curiosity.

The effort.

The follow-through.

Notice what you have been compensating for.

Indifference Is Still Information

Indifference does not always mean someone is a bad person.
It does not always mean they do not love you.

It means something is unattended.

Sometimes it means they are depleted.
Sometimes it means they are avoidant.
Sometimes it means they have become comfortable with you
carrying more than you should.

Whatever the reason, the cost is still real.

You do not need a dramatic reason to acknowledge a pattern.

You do not need proof of harm to recognize neglect.

You do not need permission to name what it is costing you.

Indifference is not neutral.

It is a direction.

It points toward disconnection.

It points toward loneliness.

It points toward a life that looks stable and feels empty.

Reflect

Write one sentence that tells the truth without minimizing it.

Something like this.

I have been paying for connection by carrying it alone.

Or this.

I have been living inside a dynamic where effort is optional for one person and required for the other.

Or this.

I keep explaining absence as normal, and it is costing me.

Do not fix it yet.

Just name it.

Naming changes the transaction.

What Comes Next

Indifference often survives because it pairs well with guilt.

Guilt keeps you trying.

Guilt keeps you quiet.

Guilt convinces you that wanting effort makes you ungrateful.

The next chapter looks at how guilt keeps people paying costs they no longer agree to.

CHAPTER EIGHT: The Cost of Guilt

Guilt is one of the most effective silencers.

It convinces you that asking for more is selfish.
That changing your mind is irresponsible.
That choosing yourself requires an apology.

Guilt keeps people paying costs they would never choose freely.
It reframes self-preservation as harm.

When Guilt Becomes a Lever

Guilt often sounds reasonable.

After everything they've done…
It's not that bad…
Other people have it worse…

Guilt minimizes your experience while amplifying obligation.
It shifts responsibility away from systems and onto individuals.

You stop asking whether the cost is fair.
You ask whether you are allowed to stop paying it.

The Trap of Being "Good"

Many people were rewarded for being agreeable.

For being helpful.

For being low-maintenance.

For being understanding.

Those traits become expectations.

Expectations turn into obligations.

Obligations rarely get renegotiated.

Continuing Without Agreement

There was a point when continuing felt automatic and stopping felt disruptive.

I said yes without checking whether I still meant it.

No one was asking too much.

I was offering too much without noticing.

The resentment came later.

Not because anyone had taken advantage of me,

but because I had kept paying for something I no longer agreed to.

Pause

Name one decision guilt has delayed or distorted for you.

Notice what guilt asks you to sacrifice.

Notice who benefits when you comply.

Consider what honesty would cost instead.

Guilt thrives in silence.

Clarity weakens it.

CHAPTER NINE: The Cost of Outsourcing Responsibility

Outsourcing responsibility feels efficient.

It sounds like trust.

It sounds like delegation.

It sounds like maturity.

In many cases, it makes sense.

Until it does not.

When Reliance Turns Into Avoidance

There is a quiet shift that happens.

You stop asking questions.

You defer decisions.

You assume someone else has it covered.

Responsibility does not disappear when you give it away.

It goes out of sight.

Out of sight does not mean out of impact.

Trust Versus Disengagement

Trust is informed engagement.

Avoidance is trust without curiosity.

Trust says, I understand enough to consent.
Avoidance says, I hope this works out.

Confidence from others can be comforting.
Comfort does not replace responsibility.

The Illusion of Safety

Believing someone else is in control reduces anxiety in the moment.
It creates the illusion of safety.

When something goes wrong, the realization hits.

You had little input.
You still carry the consequences.

Delegation and abdication are not the same.
One builds capacity.
The other erodes it.

A Familiar Pattern

There was a time when I trusted confidence over clarity.

The language sounded professional.
The tone felt certain.

I deferred.

Later, when the outcome did not align with my needs, the truth was uncomfortable.

Trust without engagement had cost me agency.

The Learning You Miss

Outsourcing responsibility also outsources learning.

You miss the chance to understand.
To ask why.
To build confidence in your judgment.

The less you engage, the less capable you feel.
The cycle reinforces itself.

Pause

Name one area where you disengaged to avoid discomfort.
Notice what decisions affect you that you no longer feel involved in.
Notice what you tell yourself to justify staying hands-off.

Consider what responsibility would look like without blame.

Responsibility is not control.
It is participation.

CHAPTER TEN: The Cost of Waiting to Feel Ready

Readiness feels responsible.

It suggests that clarity will arrive.
That confidence will settle.
That fear will fade.

So you wait.

Waiting feels safe.
It is not.

Readiness Is a Story

Most people do not delay because they are lazy.
They delay because they care.

They want to do it right.
They want to avoid regret.
They want certainty.

Calling it readiness makes fear easier to live with.
Fear still sets the timeline.

What Waiting Actually Costs

While you wait, time keeps moving.

Opportunities expire.

Momentum fades.

Circumstances change.

Avoiding a decision does not pause the outcome.
It decides for you.

Waiting feels quieter than choosing.
Quiet does not mean free.

A Moment of Recognition

There was a decision I delayed because it felt intimidating.

I told myself I needed more information.
The truth was simpler.

I was afraid of choosing wrong.

When I finally acted, the cost was higher.

Not because the choice was wrong.
Because waiting narrowed the options.

Preparation Versus Postponement

Preparation moves toward action.
Postponement circles the same questions.

One builds capacity.

The other drains energy.

Waiting without an end date is not preparation.

It is avoidance.

Pause

Name one decision you have been waiting to feel ready for.

Notice what you hope readiness will give you.

Notice what waiting is costing you right now.

Consider what one small move forward would create.

Certainty is rare.

Movement creates information.

Information creates adjustment.

Waiting creates stagnation.

INTERLUDE: What Kept Repeating

The hardest patterns to recognize are the ones that look reasonable.

They do not announce themselves as mistakes.
They do not feel reckless or careless.

They feel mature.
They feel like doing what needs to be done.

That is why they repeat.

At first, the choice feels situational.
A response to a specific moment.
A decision made under pressure.

You tell yourself it makes sense.
You tell yourself anyone would do the same.

Then the moment passes.

Later, a similar moment arrives.
The same reasoning applies.
The same response feels appropriate.
The same choice gets made.

That is how a pattern forms.

Not all at once.

Not intentionally.

Through repetition that never gets questioned.

Patterns survive because they offer short-term relief.

They remove immediate pressure.

They avoid conflict.

They create the appearance of stability.

Short-term relief feels like success.

Long-term, it becomes a loop.

You get better at coping.

You do not get freer.

The loop loses power the moment it becomes visible.

Invisibility is the only thing that sustains it.

PART III

OWN THE OUTCOME

Ownership

You do not control everything.
You are responsible for the result.

Awareness shows you the cost.
Patterns explain why it repeats.
Ownership decides what happens next.

Part I asked you to look.
Part II asked you to recognize patterns.
Part III asks you to engage.

Not with blame.
With agency.

Ownership is not about fault.
It is about influence.

This section exists to reframe responsibility as power rather than
punishment.
Because once responsibility is reclaimed, choice expands.

CHAPTER ELEVEN

Neutrality Is Over

There is no neutral ground.

Every day, something is being chosen.
Even on the days that feel like survival.
Especially on those days.

Neutrality feels passive.
It feels safe.
It feels like staying out of the way.

Neutrality is still a choice.
And it still produces outcomes.

The Illusion of "Not Choosing"

Most people do not believe they are choosing when they stay
silent or delay action.

They believe they are waiting.
They believe they are staying open.
They believe they are avoiding unnecessary conflict.

In reality, defaults are deciding.

What you do not interrupt continues.

What you tolerate compounds.

What you avoid clarifying defines the terms.

Neutrality protects comfort in the short term.

It mortgages the future.

The Cost of Staying Undefined

When you do not name what you want, other people fill in the blanks.

When you do not set boundaries, circumstances decide them.

When you do not choose direction, momentum chooses for you.

Neutrality keeps you busy without moving you forward.

It creates motion without intention.

Pause

Name one place where you have been "staying neutral."

Notice what continues because you have not interrupted it.

Notice what neutrality has cost you so far.

Consider what clarity would require instead.

Neutrality delays discomfort.

It does not eliminate it.

CHAPTER TWELVE: When Choice Isn't Available

Not every situation offers equal choice.

Pressure limits options.
Responsibility narrows freedom.
Survival demands compromise.

Acknowledging this matters.

Choice exists on a spectrum.
Pretending otherwise creates shame where compassion is needed.

There are moments when choice is constrained by survival.

By money.
By safety.
By caregiving.
By legal, relational, or economic realities that do not bend just because awareness arrives.

Not everyone has the freedom to leave, speak, quit, or disrupt without real risk.

Naming cost in these moments is not a failure of courage.
It is an act of clarity.

Constraint does not erase agency, but it does shape what agency looks like.

Pretending otherwise turns responsibility into shame instead of context.

Constrained Decisions Still Have Direction

Even when options are limited, direction still matters.

You may not choose the circumstance.
You may not choose the timing.
You may not choose the ideal outcome.

You still influence how you respond.

What you tolerate.
What you normalize.
What you plan to change when capacity returns.

Recognizing constraint is not an excuse.
It is context.

Survival Is Not Failure

There are seasons where endurance is the work.
Where staying afloat is the achievement.

Judging those seasons through the lens of freedom misses the point.

Survival is not the final goal.
It is a phase.

The danger is staying in survival mode after options expand.

Pause

Name one area where choice has felt limited.
Notice what you still influence within that constraint.
Notice what you are postponing until capacity increases.

Consider what planning for future choice could look like.

Choice does not require perfection.
It requires awareness.

CHAPTER THIRTEEN: Intentional or Not, You're Choosing

There is no neutral ground.

Every day, something is being chosen.
Even on the days that feel like survival.

Choice is often imagined as a dramatic moment.
A visible fork in the road.
A clear decision with time to think.

Most choices are quieter than that.

They happen by default.
By habit.
By momentum.

When you do not choose, life chooses for you.

The Power of Defaults

Default choices are powerful because they do not feel like choices.

You stay because leaving feels disruptive.
You agree because pushing back feels exhausting.
You continue because stopping would require explanation.

None of these moments feel dramatic.

They accumulate.
Accumulation becomes direction.
Direction becomes outcome.

Most lives are not shaped by bold decisions.
They are shaped by defaults that went unexamined.

Momentum Is Not Neutral

Momentum conserves energy in the short term.
It keeps things moving.
It avoids disruption.
It feels efficient.

Momentum does not care whether the direction still fits.

If the path was shaped by fear, obligation, or convenience,
momentum carries those values forward.

Stopping feels uncomfortable.
Stopping requires honesty.
Stopping restores agency.

A Life Built on Autopilot

There was a moment when I realized how much of my life was
running automatically.

Schedules filled themselves.

Commitments rolled forward.

Expectations went unchallenged.

Nothing felt wrong enough to stop.

The realization arrived quietly.

I was busy but not aligned.

Productive but not present.

Default choices had built a life that looked fine and felt heavy.

Pause

Name one part of your life that runs on default.

Notice what feels automatic that deserves attention.

Notice what direction momentum is reinforcing.

Consider what would change if you chose intentionally this week.

CHAPTER FOURTEEN:
Ownership Without Shame

Ownership has a reputation problem.

It is often associated with fault.
With failure.
With something you accept only after everything goes wrong.

So people avoid it.

They soften responsibility.
They explain circumstances.
They focus on what happened to them rather than what they
chose within it.

Shame makes ownership feel dangerous.

Blame Versus Ownership

Blame looks backward.
It asks who failed.
It freezes you in explanation.

Ownership looks forward.
It asks what can be changed.

Blame removes power.
Ownership restores it.

Context Matters

Most of us are doing the best we can with the tools we have.
We are coping.
We are navigating pressure.
We are managing incomplete information.

Acknowledging context does not erase responsibility.
It makes responsibility usable.

We can honor what we did not know then without surrendering
what we can do now.

A Shift That Changed Everything

There was a moment when I stopped asking who was at fault.

That question kept me stuck.

The question that changed things was simpler.

What part of this do I control now?

That question did not minimize what happened.
It redirected energy toward what was possible.

Shame Keeps Patterns Intact

Shame isolates.

It says mistakes define you.
It says acknowledgment makes you smaller.

Ownership integrates.
It allows experience to become information rather than identity.

Avoiding ownership does not protect you.
It preserves the pattern.

Pause

Name one place where you avoid ownership to avoid shame.
Notice what outcome you keep explaining instead of addressing.
Notice what responsibility feels heavy because it feels personal.

Consider what would shift if shame was removed from the equation.

Ownership without cruelty creates movement.

CHAPTER FIFTEEN: Money Is a Mirror

Money is rarely just about money.

It reflects safety.
Control.
Fear.
Worth.
Trust.

Numbers tell a story.
They are not the whole story.

More Money Does Not Fix Patterns

Many people believe financial stress would disappear with more income.

Sometimes that is true.
Often, more money magnifies existing patterns.

Avoidance becomes easier.
Poor boundaries become more expensive.
Unclear priorities carry greater consequences.

Money exposes patterns.
It does not erase them.

Avoidance Is Information

Ignoring balances.
Delaying conversations.
Avoiding statements.

These behaviors are not laziness.
They signal discomfort.

Discomfort left unexamined becomes costly.

A Moment of Clarity

There was a time when I avoided looking closely at my finances.

Not because I did not care.
Because it made me anxious.

Avoidance did not reduce the anxiety.
It multiplied it.

Looking honestly did not fix everything.
It restored agency.

Money and Boundaries

Money reflects boundaries.

How often you say yes when you should say no.

How often you rescue others at your expense.

How often spending soothes instead of solves.

These choices make sense in the moment.

They still shape outcomes.

Pause

Name what you feel when you think about money.

Notice where you avoid looking closely.

Notice what patterns repeat regardless of income.

Consider what awareness would change before any number does.

Logic Is Not the Driver

Money decisions are rarely made in calm conditions.

They are made under stress.

Under urgency.

Under emotion.

Logic participates.

Emotion drives.

Understanding that changes how you approach money.

Reflect

Name one financial pattern you have normalized.

Notice how it shows up and what it protects you from feeling.

Notice what it costs you long term in peace or options.

Consider what one honest look would interrupt.

Money is not a verdict.

It is feedback.

INTERLUDE: Own the Outcome

Owning the outcome does not mean controlling every variable.

It means staying engaged with the result.
It means noticing where your influence exists.
It means asking better questions instead of assigning blame.
It means participating even when it feels uncomfortable.

Ownership is not heavy.
Avoidance is.

When you stop waiting for permission, something shifts.

Decisions feel clearer.
Boundaries feel firmer.
Energy feels more intentional.

Owning the outcome does not make life easier.
It makes it yours.

PART IV

PAYING FORWARD

Legacy

What you learn late does not have to be paid for twice.

Legacy is what's left behind.
It is what remains after the choices are made,
after the patterns settle,
after the urgency fades.

But legacy is not only a future concern.
It is being built while life is still happening.

What you leave behind is shaped by what you repeat now.
By what you interrupt.
By what you allow to continue without question.

Up to this point, the work has been about awareness and
ownership.
Seeing the cost.
Recognizing the pattern.
Reclaiming influence.

This section is about what remains.

Because once a cost is visible, it becomes transferable.

If it is not examined, it is inherited.

If it is not interrupted, it becomes expectation.

The most meaningful costs are rarely eliminated.

They are carried forward or redirected.

Redirected away from silence that teaches others what to tolerate.

Away from comfort that quietly becomes precedent.

Away from cycles that survive because no one named them.

Legacy forms through repetition.

Through what becomes normal.

Through what stops being questioned.

It shows up in how pressure is handled.

How conflict is repaired or avoided.

How money is discussed, ignored, or feared.

How boundaries are modeled when they are inconvenient.

This section is not about perfection.

It is about responsibility.

Because what you absorb without examination does not disappear.

It settles.

It teaches.
It shapes.

Some lessons cost more because they were learned late.
That does not mean they have to be paid for twice.

Paying forward means absorbing certain costs now
so they do not compound later.

It means choosing awareness over convenience.
Interruption over endurance.
Engagement over autopilot.

Part IV is not about having everything resolved.
It is about being conscious of what you are leaving behind.

What follows looks directly at cycles, inheritance, growth, and
discernment.
Not to assign blame.
To clarify responsibility.

Legacy is not built in one moment.
It is built in what repeats.

And once you see what is being charged quietly,
you stop paying blindly.

CHAPTER SIXTEEN: Breaking the Cycle Costs More Up Front

Patterns do not repeat because people want them to.

They repeat because they are familiar.

Because they feel survivable.

Because changing them requires effort before it offers relief.

Effort feels expensive.

Breaking a cycle almost always costs more at the beginning.

More energy.

More discomfort.

More awareness.

Staying where you are costs less up front.

That difference matters.

Familiar Is Efficient

Cycles are efficient.

They do not require new thinking.

They do not demand difficult conversations.

They allow you to operate on instinct and history.

Efficiency feels like relief when you are tired.

Efficiency built on dysfunction drains over time.

Staying in a cycle rarely feels dramatic.
It feels manageable.

Manageable is where many people stay the longest.

The Lie of Later

Many people tell themselves they will break the cycle later.

When life calms down.
When there is more time.
When there is more money.
When there is more support.

Cycles do not loosen when life gets easier.
They tighten.

They were built to function under pressure.

A Choice That Felt Heavy

There was a moment when choosing differently felt disruptive.

It would have been easier to stay consistent.
To avoid the conversation.
To maintain the pattern.

Breaking it meant discomfort now.
Staying meant paying later.

That distinction changed how I saw cost.

Grief Is Part of the Price

Breaking a cycle often includes grief.

Grief for what should have been different.
Grief for what you did not receive.
Grief for the ease you hoped change would bring.

Ignoring grief does not make the process lighter.
Naming it makes the work honest.

Pause

Take a moment before moving on.

Name one cycle you recognize but hesitate to interrupt.
Notice what breaking it would cost immediately.
Notice what staying has already cost you over time.

Consider which cost you are more willing to keep paying.

Choosing long-term freedom is not impulsive.
It is intentional.

CHAPTER SEVENTEEN: The Cost of What Becomes Normal

Legacy is not created by what you intend.
It is created by what becomes normal.

Most people think legacy is something you leave behind later.
Something attached to age.
Something that arrives once the work is finished.

That is not how it forms.

Legacy is built quietly, while life is happening.
While decisions are made under pressure.
While exhaustion shapes reactions.
While silence fills space that honesty never reaches.

What repeats becomes instruction.

Normal Is a Teacher

People do not learn first from explanation.
They learn from exposure.

They learn what matters by watching what gets protected.
They learn what can be ignored by watching what is tolerated.
They learn how much effort is expected by watching who carries the weight when things get uncomfortable.

Normal teaches faster than intention ever will.

If emotional absence is normal, people adapt to it.
If silence is normal, people learn to swallow.
If over-functioning is normal, people learn that care is something
one person provides while others receive.

No one announces this lesson.
It just settles.

The Cost of Unexamined Normal

Unexamined normal is expensive because it does not look
harmful.
It looks familiar.
It looks stable.
It looks like getting through the day.

You normalize what you cannot stop long enough to question.

Patterns become invisible once they work well enough to keep
things moving.
Function replaces alignment.
Endurance replaces repair.

Over time, what was once a choice becomes expectation.
That expectation gets inherited.

What Gets Passed Down Without Words

People often ask what they are teaching by staying.

By working harder.

By holding it together.

The more important question is this.

What are you teaching by not naming cost.

You teach others how to treat effort.

You teach them how conflict gets handled.

You teach them whether care is reciprocal or assumed.

You teach them whether exhaustion is normal.

Whether self-erasure is maturity.

Whether silence is safer than truth.

No speech is required.

The lesson arrives through repetition.

Comfort as Curriculum

Comfort is one of the most powerful teachers.

Not comfort as rest.

Comfort as avoidance.

When discomfort is consistently avoided, people learn that honesty is dangerous.

When tension is smoothed over instead of addressed, people learn that stability matters more than truth.
When imbalance is carried quietly, people learn that fairness is optional.

Comfort that comes at the expense of clarity becomes precedent. Precedent is how systems survive without scrutiny.

The Invisible Handoff

There is a moment most people miss.

The moment when what you have been carrying stops being temporary and starts becoming instructional.

When children stop noticing what you say and start noticing how you live.
When teams stop responding to values and start responding to behavior.
When partners stop hearing requests and start trusting patterns.

This is not about blame.
It is about awareness.

You cannot interrupt what you do not see being handed forward.

Breaking Normal Is Disruptive

Interrupting normal rarely feels clean.

It introduces tension where quiet once existed.

It raises questions that were never meant to be asked.

It changes expectations without asking permission.

Breaking normal costs energy up front.

Staying inside it costs agency over time.

That is the trade.

Most people delay interruption because the system still works.

They wait for a breaking point.

They wait for justification.

Legacy does not wait for justification.

It forms anyway.

Pause

Name one thing in your life that has become normal without being chosen.

Notice how long it has been that way.

Notice who benefits from it staying unnamed.

Notice what it quietly teaches.

Choosing What Gets Carried Forward

Legacy is not about removing all cost.

It is about deciding which costs are worth passing on.

Some costs build resilience.
Some costs build fear.
Some costs teach discernment.
Some costs teach silence.

The work is not perfection.
The work is selection.

You choose what effort means.
You choose what repair looks like.
You choose what happens when something feels misaligned.

Those choices become structure.

Responsibility Without Weight

Responsibility here is not about pressure.
It is about clarity.

Once you see what has been normalized, you can decide whether
it deserves to continue.

You may still choose stability.
You may still choose patience.
You may still choose endurance.

The difference is consent.

Chosen costs strengthen.
Inherited costs drain.

Reflect

Finish this sentence honestly.

What I allow to stay unexamined becomes someone else's normal.

Sit with what comes up.
No fixing.
No action plan.

Just awareness.

What Comes Next

The next chapter looks directly at what the next generation should never have to unlearn.

Not because you did everything wrong.
Because awareness gives you the chance to interrupt what no longer needs to repeat.

CHAPTER EIGHTEEN: What the Next Generation Shouldn't Have to Unlearn

Every generation inherits something.

Not just traditions or habits.
Beliefs.
Unspoken rules.
Expectations around money, love, conflict, and worth.

Some inheritances are strengths.
Others are debts.

The most costly ones are the ones no one names.

Learning Without Language

Children learn before they understand.

They absorb tone.
They notice patterns.
They internalize what feels normal.

They learn how conflict is handled by watching what gets avoided.
They learn what money means by observing stress or silence.
They learn what love looks like by noticing what is tolerated.

No lesson is neutral.

Normalization Is Powerful

Struggle becomes invisible when it is constant.
Tension feels expected when it is familiar.
One-sided sacrifice feels like duty when it goes unnamed.

Children adapt to what surrounds them.
They do not question it.

They build their understanding of normal from it.

A Moment of Awareness

There was a moment when I realized my reactions were being watched.

Not my explanations.
My responses.

What I normalized was teaching more than anything I said.

That realization sharpened every choice that followed.

Patterns Speak Louder Than Intention

The next generation inherits patterns.

The way pressure is handled.

The way repair happens.

The way self-talk sounds in difficult moments.

Guilt does not help this realization.

Honesty does.

Pause

Name one pattern that was normalized for you growing up.

Notice what you had to unlearn later.

Notice how it still tries to show up under stress.

Consider what you want to normalize instead.

Language Changes Weight

One of the most meaningful gifts is language.

Language for emotions.

Language for boundaries.

Language for money.

What is named becomes manageable.

What remains unspoken becomes heavy.

CHAPTER NINETEEN: Building While Learning

There is a belief that keeps people frozen.

The belief that understanding must come first.

That clarity is a prerequisite.

That growth should look clean.

Real life does not work that way.

People build while uncertain.

They heal while still hurting.

They choose while afraid.

That does not invalidate progress.

Perfection Is Not the Entry Point

If you waited until you felt ready, nothing meaningful would begin.

Conversations would remain unspoken.

Patterns would stay intact.

Change would be postponed indefinitely.

Waiting feels safer.

Waiting has a cost.

Imperfect Foundations Still Hold

Building while learning means accepting imperfection.

Some decisions will need revision.

Some choices will look naïve later.

Those choices were made in motion.

Motion matters.

A Vulnerable Season

There was a season when building felt exposed.

Answers were incomplete.

Confidence wavered.

Certainty was absent.

Continuing anyway changed everything.

Progress does not require polish.

It requires presence.

Mistakes Become Data

Mistakes stop being identity when shame is removed.

They become information.

What drained you teaches you.

What failed reveals something.

What cost more than expected sharpens awareness.

Pause

Name one place where you demand mastery before movement.

Notice what you are postponing until you feel ready.

Notice what that delay costs you in momentum or peace.

Consider what learning in motion would look like.

CHAPTER TWENTY: The Cost Worth Paying

Every life costs something.

Awareness does not change that.
Awareness sharpens choice.

Unconscious Spending

For much of life, costs are absorbed without consent.

Time because it feels expected.
Energy because it feels responsible.
Silence because it feels safer.

Awareness changes that equation.

Some Costs Are Investments

Not all costs are harmful.

Growth costs discomfort.
Healing costs honesty.
Alignment costs change.

These costs build capacity.
They move you forward.

Discernment Is the Skill

The work is learning the difference.

Between spending that builds and spending that depletes.
Between patience and avoidance.
Between sacrifice and self-erosion.

Discernment compounds.

A Different Way to Choose

There will still be moments of comfort.
Delay.
Familiar paths.

Awareness does not demand perfection.
It provides direction.

Pause

Name one cost you are paying unconsciously right now.
Notice what it asks of you each week.
Notice whether it builds you or drains you.

Consider what awareness would change first.

Ownership is engagement.
Engagement changes outcomes.

Closing: What Remains

At some point, urgency fades.

Not because everything is resolved.

Because awareness changes how pressure is handled.

You stop asking only what went wrong.

You start noticing what is ongoing.

What keeps charging quietly.

What still asks for payment.

Attention shifts.

Toward patterns instead of moments.

Toward accumulation instead of events.

Toward what is being funded without consent.

This book was never about avoiding cost.

Every life costs something.

Growth costs.

Healing costs.

Stability costs.

So does silence.

So does delay.

So does choosing comfort when alignment asks for more.

The difference is not whether cost exists.

The difference is whether it stays invisible.

When cost is unnamed, it compounds.

When it is named, it becomes negotiable.

When it is negotiable, choice returns.

That is what awareness actually gives you.

Not certainty.

Not guarantees.

Consent.

You begin to see where your time is going.

Where your energy is being spent.

Where responsibility has turned into depletion.

Where patience has turned into avoidance.

Where survival became a long-term strategy without being questioned.

This is not about fixing everything.

It is about interrupting what no longer deserves automatic payment.

Legacy lives here too.

Not as an obligation.

As a consequence.

What you normalize becomes instruction.

What you interrupt becomes possibility.

What you continue without examination becomes structure.

This is what remains.

Not a finished product.

A practiced awareness.

Not a perfect life.

A conscious one.

You will still face decisions without clarity.

You will still feel pressure.

You will still choose comfort sometimes.

The difference now is this.

Cost does not get to hide.

Not in habit.

Not in silence.

Not in default.

You get to pause long enough to ask,

What am I paying for.

What is this building.

What is this costing me over time.

Is this a price I still agree to.

Because once you see the receipt clearly, you stop paying blindly.

You start choosing what is worth the investment.

This cost me something.

This cost you something, too.

What follows does not have to cost as much.

Before You Go

Naming the cost does not undo it.

Awareness does not return what was spent.
It does not repair the years lived on borrowed energy,
the choices made out of obligation,
or the silence that kept things functioning longer than they
should have.

Clarity is not resolution.
It is interruption.

Once something is seen, it cannot be unseen.
What felt survivable begins to feel heavy.
What once passed as normal starts asking questions it never
asked before.

This is not the moment where everything changes.
It is the moment where pretending becomes harder.

If you are uncomfortable here, that makes sense.
This is the space between knowing and choosing.
Between recognition and movement.
Between the life you have been living
and the one you are no longer sure you can keep living the same
way.

This book ends here.

The next one begins in the middle.

www.ingramcontent.com/pod-product-compliance
Lightning Source LLC
Chambersburg PA
CBHW070719130626
46553CB00005B/2063